KIDS' SONGS FROM CONTEMPORARY MUSICALS

15 Songs from 8 Musicals

To access companion recorded accompaniments online, visit:
www.halleonard.com/mylibrary

Enter Code
8046-3014-2782-5422

ISBN 978-1-4803-9522-0

HAL•LEONARD® CORPORATION

7777 W. BLUEMOUND RD. P.O. BOX 13819 MILWAUKEE, WI 53213

Visit Hal Leonard Online at
www.halleonard.com

CONTENTS

Pianists on the recording: [1] John Reed
[2] Lisa Despain

COUNTING DOWN TO CHRISTMAS

from *A Christmas Story - The Musical*

Words and Music by Benj Pasek
and Justin Paul

neigh-bors bought a nine-foot danc-ing Santa for their roof.

But this year, who wants an-oth-er wool cap?

This year, I want a gift I want to un-wrap and I'm _____ _____ run-ning out of time. _____ 'Cause it's

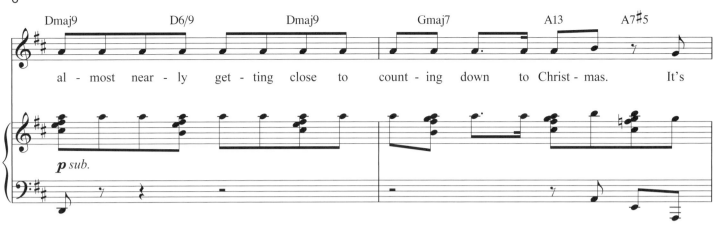

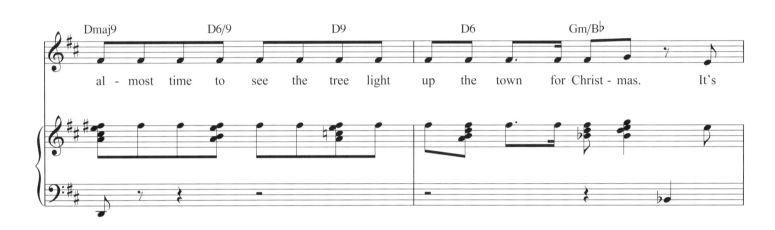

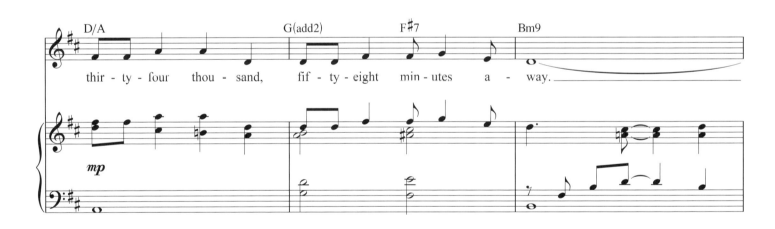

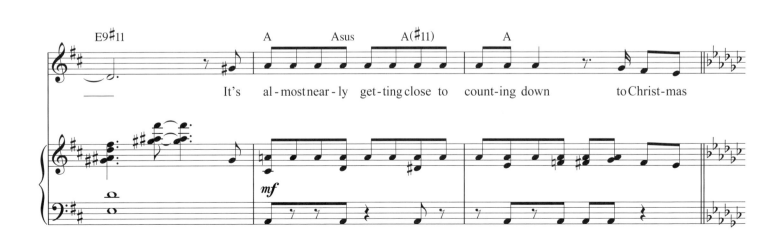

RED RYDER® CARBINE ACTION BB GUN

from *A Christmas Story - The Musical*

Words and Music by Benj Pasek
and Justin Paul

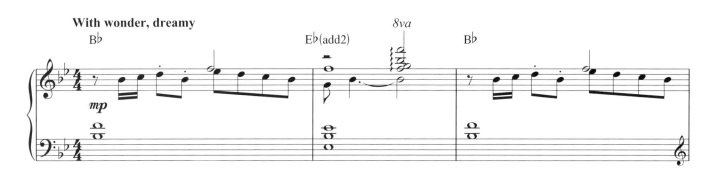

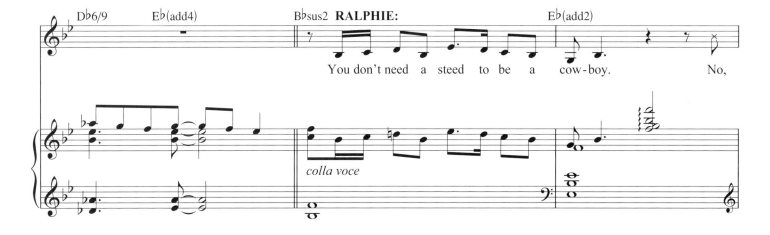

RALPHIE:
You don't need a steed to be a cow-boy. No,

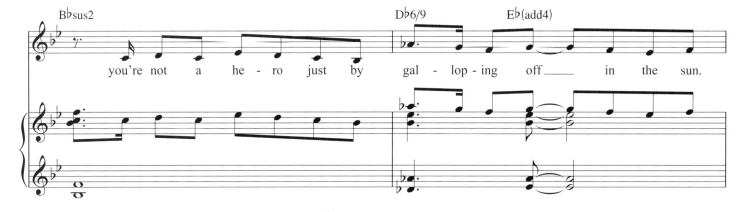

you're not a he - ro just by gal - lop - ing off____ in the sun.

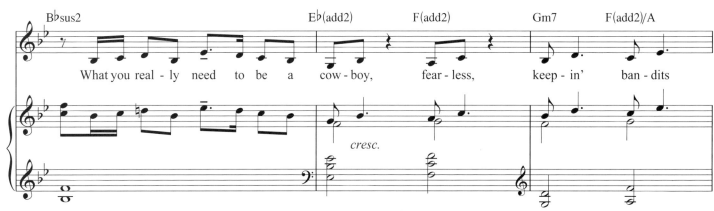

What you real - ly need to be a cow - boy, fear - less, keep - in' ban - dits

SOMEWHERE HOVERING OVER INDIANA

from *A Christmas Story - The Musical*

Words and Music by Benj Pasek
and Justin Paul

WHAT IF
from *The Addams Family*

Music and Lyrics by
Andrew Lippa

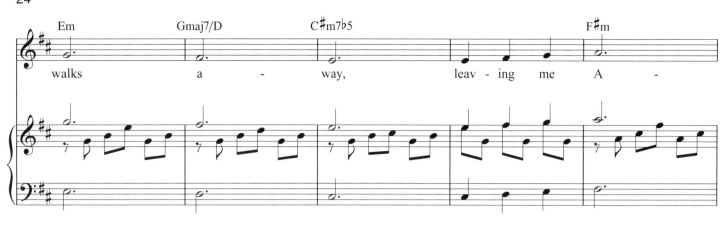

walks a - way, leav - ing me A -

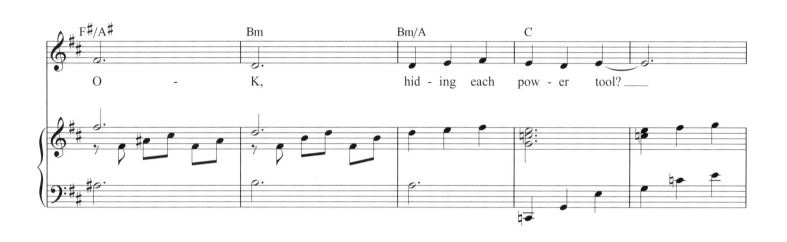

O - K, hid - ing each pow - er tool? ___

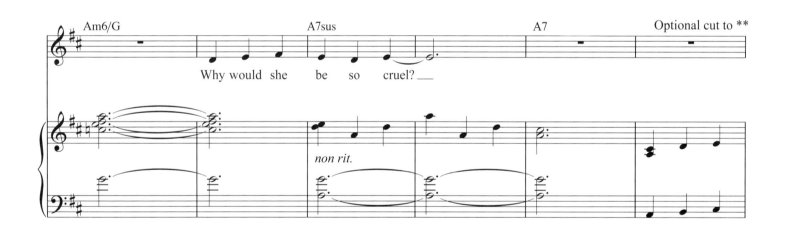

Why would she be so cruel? ___

non rit.

Optional cut to **

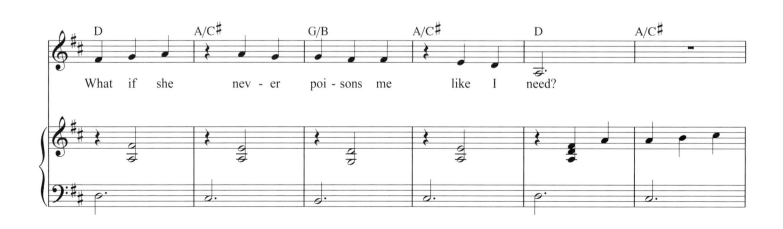

What if she nev - er poi - sons me like I need?

Who can I turn to? Where's the soul who can make me whole

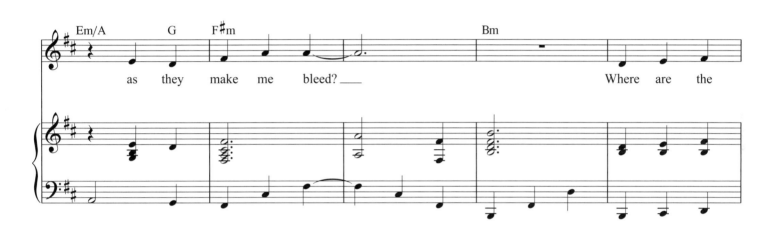

as they make me bleed? ___ Where are the

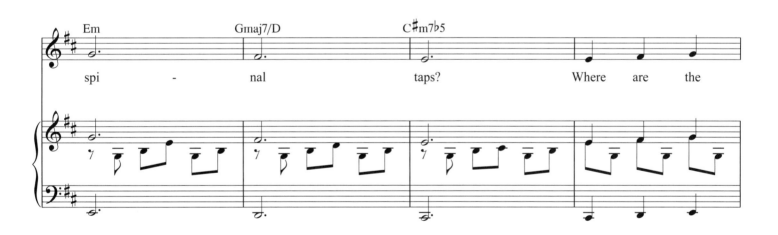

spi - nal taps? Where are the

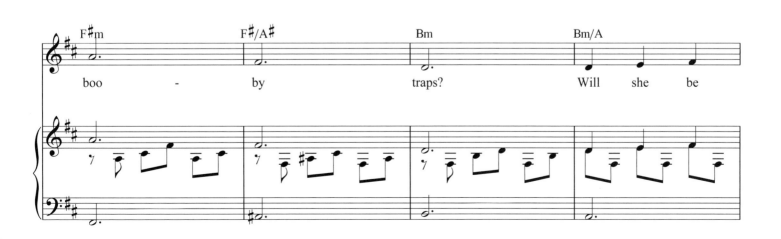

boo - by traps? Will she be

DO YOU WANT TO BUILD A SNOWMAN?

from Disney's Animated Feature *Frozen*

Music and Lyrics by Kristen Anderson-Lopez
and Robert Lopez

Moderate-rhythmic but expressive

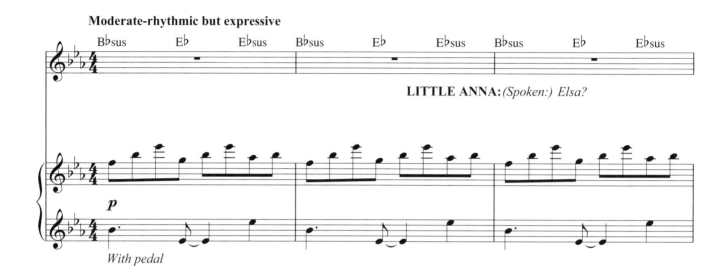

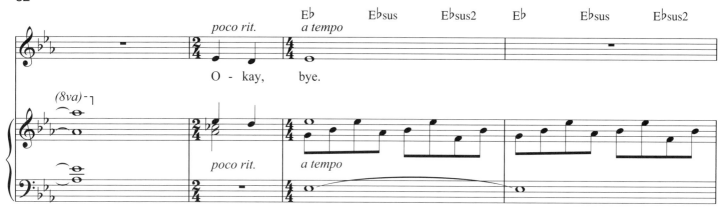

O - kay, bye.

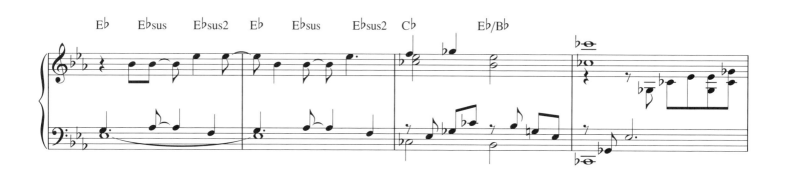

A little faster

Do you want to build a snow - man?   Or ride our bikes a - round the

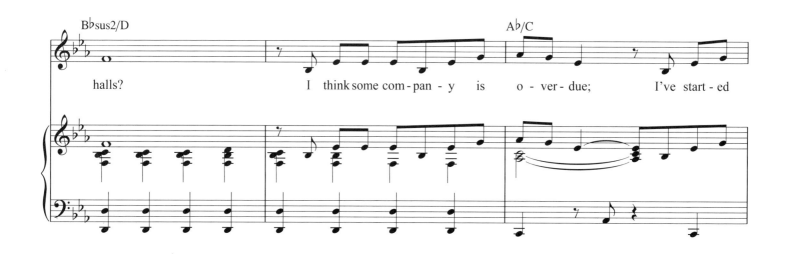

halls?   I think some com - pan - y is o - ver - due; I've start - ed

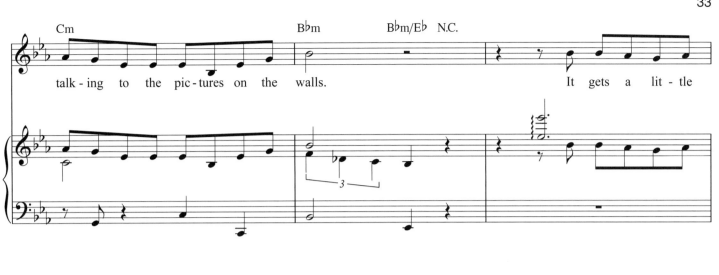

talk-ing to the pic-tures on the walls. It gets a lit-tle

lone-ly, all these emp-ty rooms, just watch-ing the hours tick

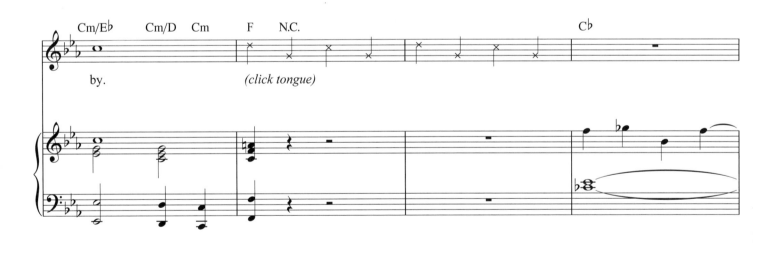

by. (click tongue)

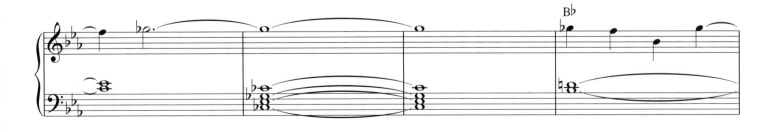

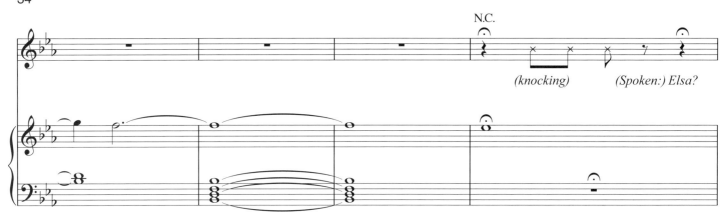

(knocking) (Spoken:) Elsa?

A little slower, tenderly

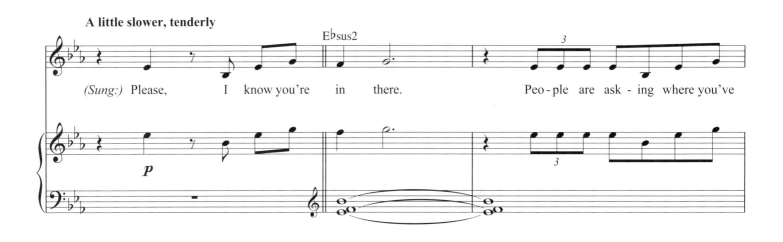

E♭sus2

(Sung:) Please, I know you're in there. Peo - ple are ask - ing where you've

B♭sus2/D A♭/C

been. They say, "Have cour - age," and I'm try - ing to; I'm right out

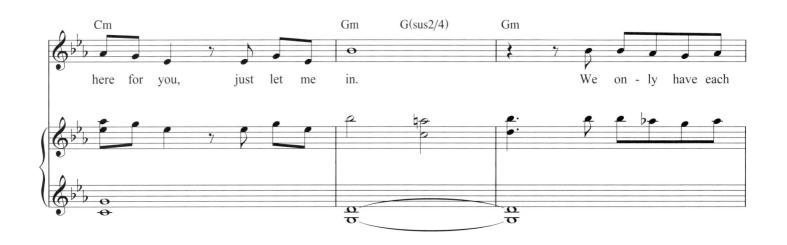

Cm Gm G(sus2/4) Gm

here for you, just let me in. We on - ly have each

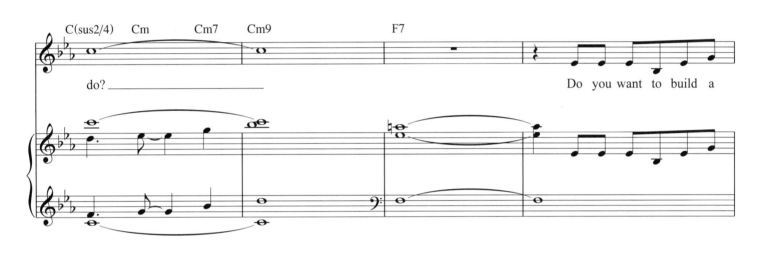

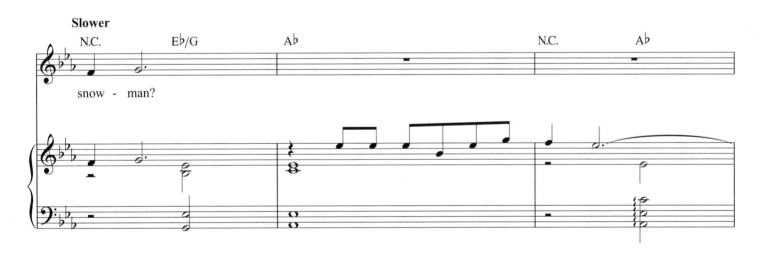

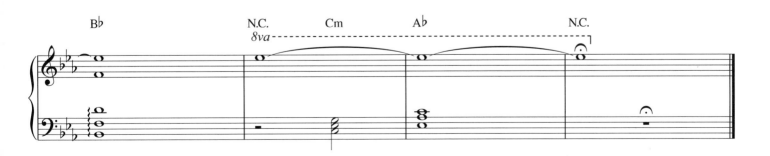

PART OF YOUR WORLD

from Walt Disney's *The Little Mermaid - A Broadway Musical*

Music by Alan Menken
Lyrics by Howard Ashman

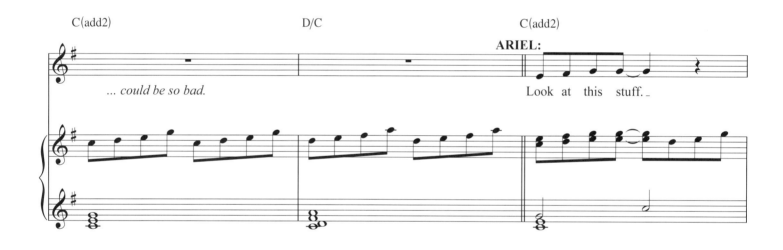

gadg - ets and giz - mos a - plen - ty. I've got who - zits and what - zits ga -

lore. You want thing - a - ma - bobs? I've got twen - ty. But who

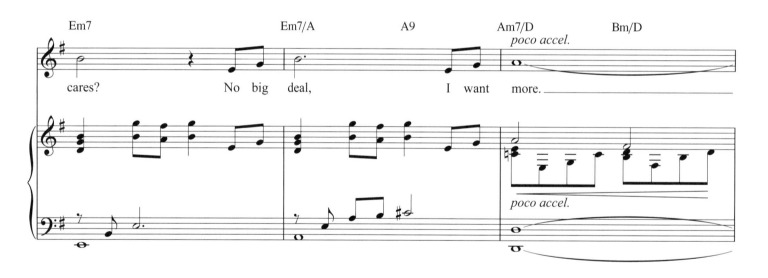

cares? No big deal, I want more.

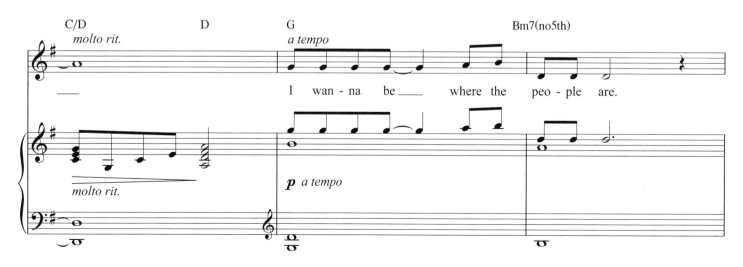

I wan - na be____ where the peo - ple are.

40

SHE'S IN LOVE

from Walt Disney's *The Little Mermaid - A Broadway Musical*

Music by Alan Menken
Lyrics by Glenn Slater

1960s Girl-group Pop beat

MERSISTER:

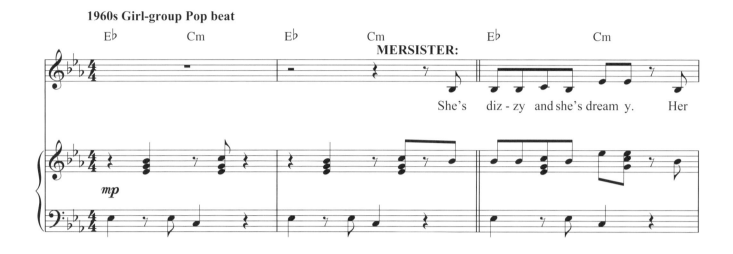

She's diz-zy and she's dream-y. Her

head's up in the foam. Her eyes have gone all gleam-y, it's like

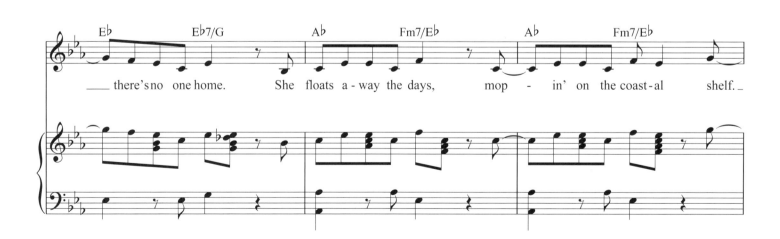

there's no one home. She floats a-way the days, mop-in' on the coast-al shelf.

THE WORLD ABOVE
from Walt Disney's *The Little Mermaid - A Broadway Musical*

Music by Alan Menken
Lyrics by Glenn Slater

Steadily, with excitement, in 2

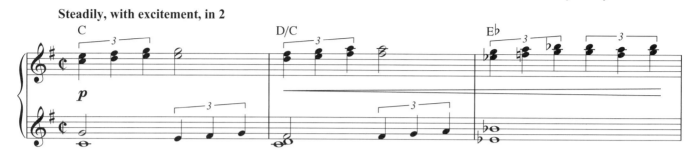

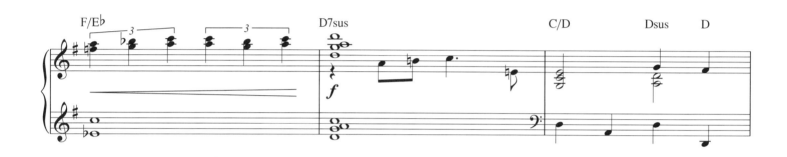

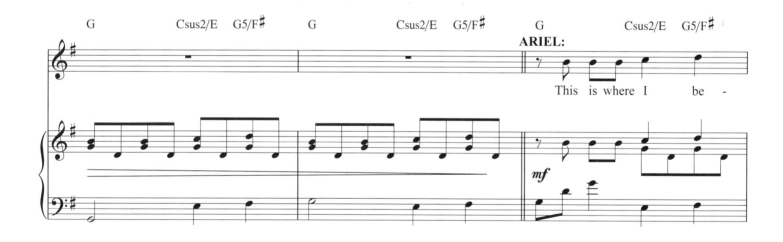

ARIEL:
This is where I be-

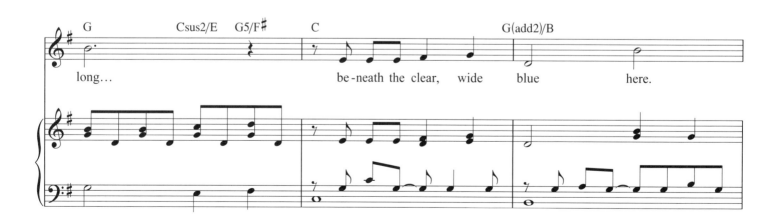

long... be-neath the clear, wide blue here.

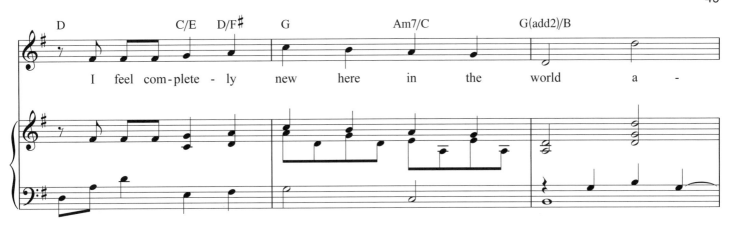

I feel com-plete-ly new here in the world a -

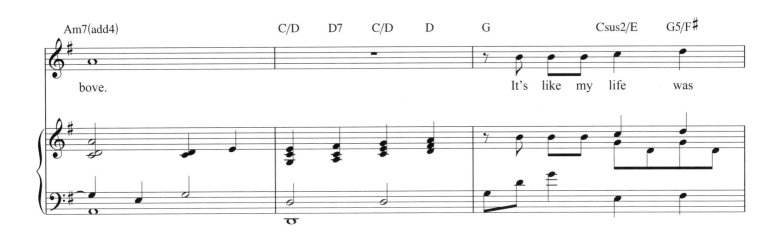

bove. It's like my life was

wrong. And some-how now at last I'm

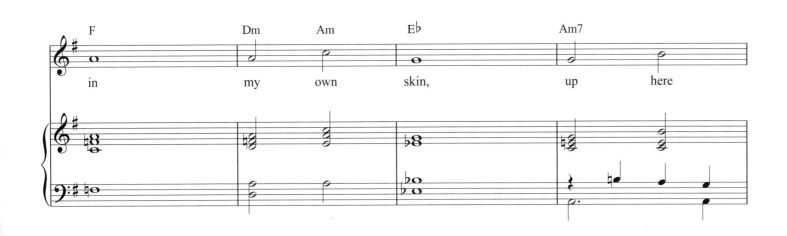

in my own skin, up here

feels so right here, warm as

love. Life seems to be al-most call-ing to me from this

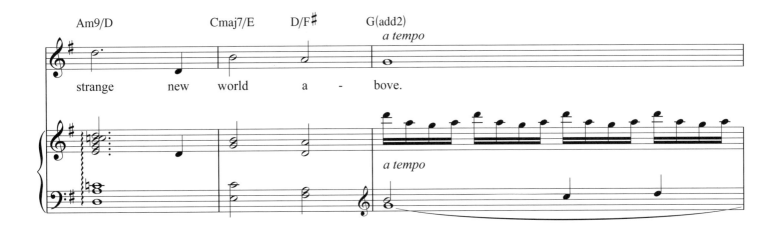

strange new world a - bove.

GREEN EGGS AND HAM

from *Seussical the Musical*

Words by Lynn Ahrens and Dr. Seuss
Music by Stephen Flaherty

Bright Swing! ($\quarternote$ = 208)

I KNOW IT'S TODAY
from *Shrek the Musical*

Words and Music by David Lindsey-Abaire
and Jeanine Tesori

The song, first sung by Young Fiona then Teen Fiona, then the adult Fiona, has been adapted as a solo.
Original key is one step higher.

hair." ___ So I know ___ he'll ap - pear _____ 'cause there are

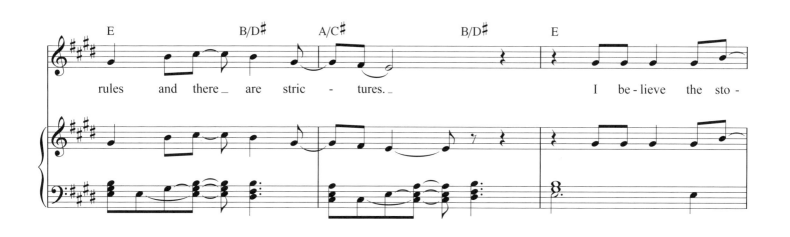

rules and there _ are stric - tures. ___ I be - lieve the sto -

- ry - books _ I read ___ by can - dle - light. ___ My white

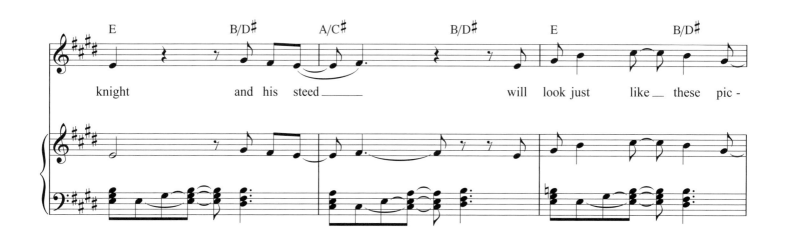

knight and his steed _____ will look just like __ these pic -

HOME
from the Broadway Musical *Wonderland*

Music by Frank Wildhorn
Lyrics by Jack Murphy

NAUGHTY
from *Matilda the Musical*

Words and Music by
Tim Minchin

Ro - me - o and Ju - li - et: 'twas writ - ten in the stars be - fore they e - ven met

that love and fate and a touch of stu - pid - i - ty would

rob them of their hope of liv - ing hap - pi - ly. The end - ings are of - ten a

lit - tle bit go - ry. *(Finger snaps)* I won - der why they did - n't just change their sto - ry.

you have to put it right.

In the slip of a bolt, there's a ti - ny re - volt. The see of a war

___ in the creak___ of a floor - board. A storm can be - gin with the flap of a wing.

The ti - ni - est mite___ packs the might - i - est sting. Ev - 'ry day

QUIET
from *Matilda the Musical*

Words and Music by
Tim Minchin

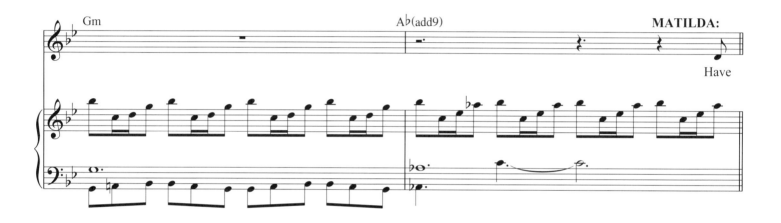

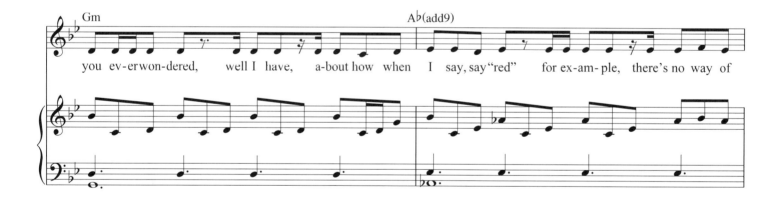

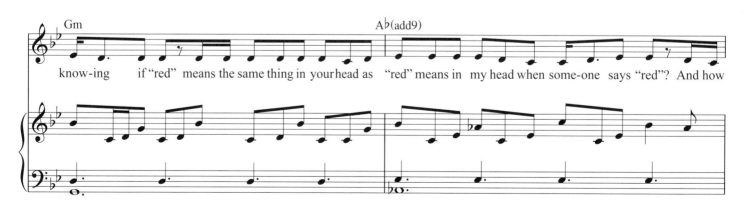

Gm   Ab(add9)

if we are trav-el-ing   at al-most the speed of light   and we're hold-ing a light,   that light would still

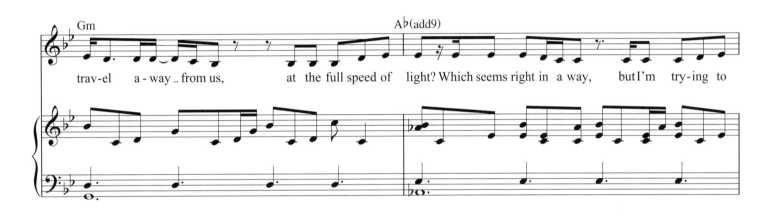

Gm   Ab(add9)

trav-el a-way _ from us,   at the full speed of light? Which seems right in a way,   but I'm try-ing to

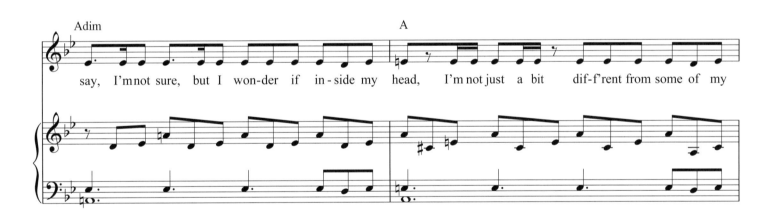

Adim   A

say, I'm not sure, but I won-der if in-side my head,   I'm not just a bit   dif-f'rent from some of my

Bb   G7/B   C   A/C#

friends. These an-swers that come in-to my mind un - bid-den. These stor-ies de-liv-ered   to me ful-ly

82

REVOLTING CHILDREN
from *Matilda the Musical*

Words and Music by
Tim Minchin

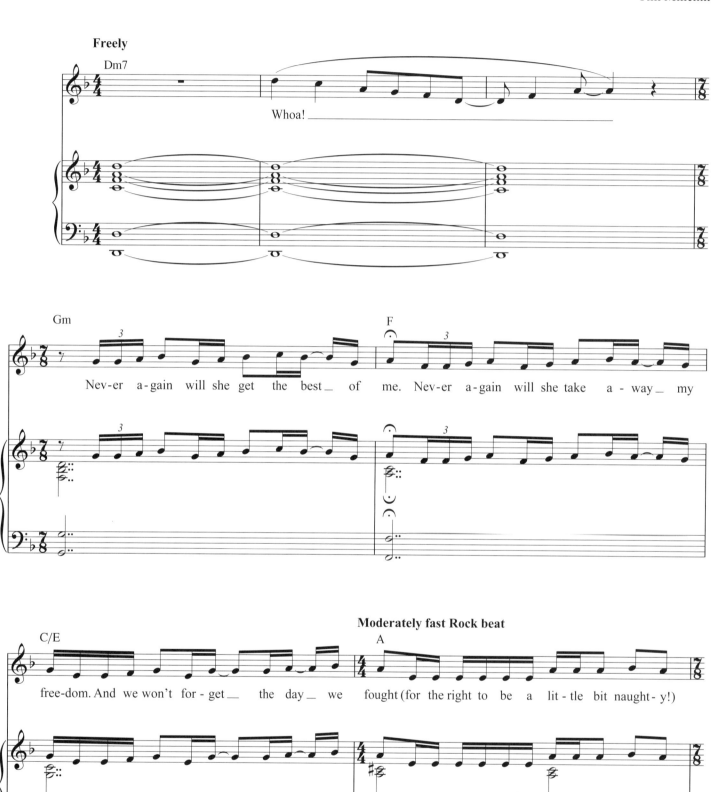

Adapted as a solo. Original key: one step higher.

WHEN I GROW UP
from *Matilda the Musical*

Words and Music by
Tim Minchin